PIANO • VOCAL • GUITAR

# DANIEL BEDINGFIELD GOTT...US

G00015407

## CONTENTS

ISBN 0-634-06526-2

HAL•LEONARD® CORPORATION

7777 W. Bluemound Rd. P.O. Box 13819 Milwaukee, WI 53213

Visit Hal Leonard Online at
www.halleonard.com

# BLOWN IT AGAIN

Words and Music by DANIEL BEDINGFIELD
and JAHAZIEL ELLIOT

Gone and lost my one true friend. If I _____ can't stop it, it's gon - na end. _____

I've done it, I've blown it a - gain. _____ Fi - nal - ly I'm ___ see - ing clear - ly.

I'm writ - ing this so you can hear me. How did I get it in my head that

you could do me wrong? No. Since I got to know you bet - ter,

I found that I was glad I met ya. Why did I lis-ten to those lies when

you were stand-ing there ___ for me? ___ (2.) ___ } Why did I nev-

F#m(maj7)

-er tell ___ you? ___ Why did I not ___ say? ___ Why did I

F#m7

F#m6

push it a-way? ___ Hey. ___ Why did I nev-

F#m

*Rap Lyrics*

I'm sorry I said it. My motor mouth done did it again,
Exceeding the speed limit, and now I'm feeling it.
I'm knee deep in it, ready to roll
Like a Jeep with the keys in it, so give me three minutes.
'Cause I admit it; I was wrong, with no right to expect.
Maybe you might just accept my apology,
Even though it feels funny.
'Cause when the penny dropped, I'm like, "Oh my gosh! I killed Kenny!"

I can't believe I'd end up dissin' a friend.
Man, I should have known better than to listen to them,
With their see-through, poisonous lies. Deceitful!
Made you the last one on my list to speak to, yeah,
Sticks and stones break bones and kill.
Word wounds take long to heal.
I was wrong for real, and I ain't even gon' try and deny, *(To Song)*

# JAMES DEAN
## (I Wanna Know)

Words and Music by
DANIEL BEDINGFIELD

12

Bm7       G/B

I wan - na know   if you're

G       D   Bm7       G/B       G

bus - y.       I wan - na know   if you're do - in' an - y - thing __ to - night.

# GOTTA GET THRU THIS

Words and Music by
DANIEL BEDINGFIELD

# IF I'M NOT MADE FOR YOU
## (If You're Not the One)

Words and Music by
DANIEL BEDINGFIELD

**Slow Ballad**

# HE DON'T LOVE YOU
# LIKE I LOVE YOU

Words and Music by
DANIEL BEDINGFIELD

Moderately fast

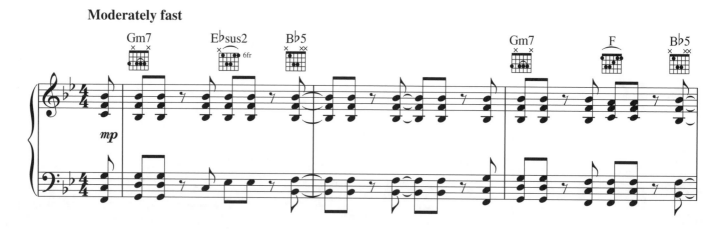

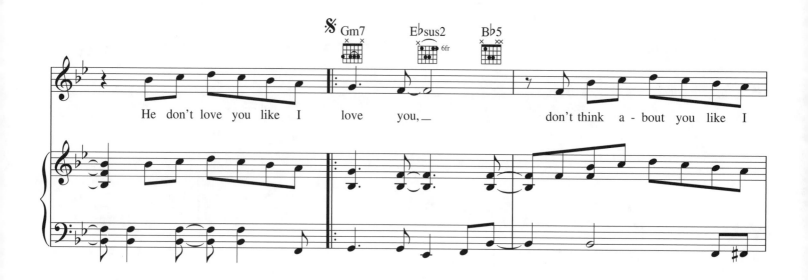

He don't love you like I love you, ___ don't think a-bout you like I

think a-bout ___ you. He don't wan-na have your chil-dren. ___

# I CAN'T READ YOU

Words and Music by
DANIEL BEDINGFIELD

**Moderately fast**

I'm nev-er shy,___ but this___
Like you so much___ I'm act-

___ is dif-f'rent. I can't ex-plain___ the way___ I'm feel-in' to-night.___
-in' stu-pid. I can't play the game.___ I'm all___ in-tense___ and a-live.___

I'm los-ing con-trol___ of my heart.___
I'm los-in' con-trol___ of my heart.___

38

# FRIDAY

Words and Music by
DANIEL BEDINGFIELD

# HONEST QUESTIONS

Words and Music by
DANIEL BEDINGFIELD

**Slowly, expressively**

Can you see ___ the hon-est ques-tions in ___ my heart ___ this hour? ___

I'm op-'ning like ___ a flow - er ___ to the rain. ___ And do you know ___

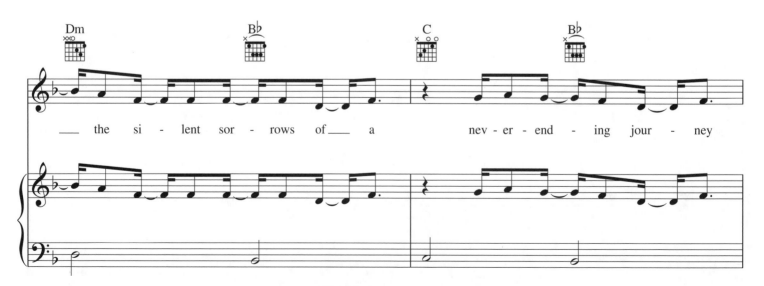

___ the si - lent sor - rows of ___ a nev - er - end - ing jour - ney

# GIRLFRIEND

Words and Music by
DANIEL BEDINGFIELD

**Moderately**

Girl - friend,

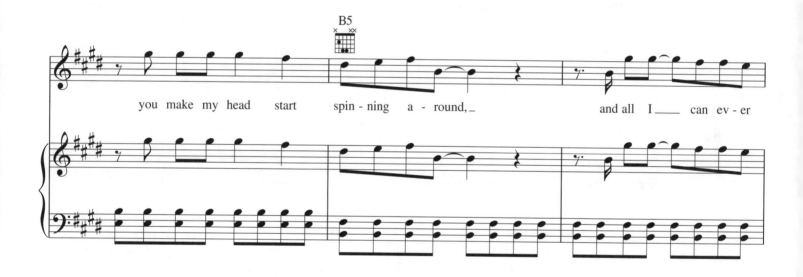

you make my head start spin - ning a - round,___ and all I ___ can ev - er

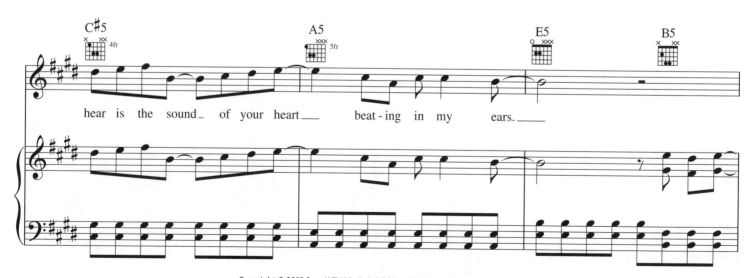

hear is the sound_ of your heart ___ beat - ing in my ears. ___

# WITHOUT THE GIRL

Words and Music by
DANIEL BEDINGFIELD

Her ma - ma told____ me if I want her I've____ got - ta

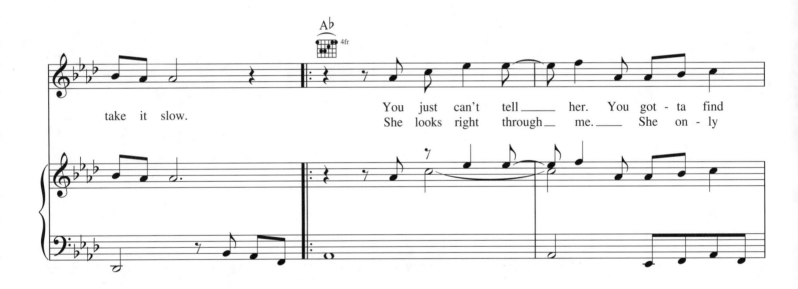

take it slow.

You just can't tell____ her. You got - ta find
She looks right through____ me.____ She on - ly

oth - er ways to let her know.
ev - er thought of us as friends,

But I don't un -
but I'll keep hold -

# INFLATE MY EGO

Words and Music by
DANIEL BEDINGFIELD

Rang her up and her fa-ther said, "She's gone.___ You're too __ late, boy,__

know how much___ I love_____ her._____

There's no way I can feel a - bout_ it, 'cause I don't e - ven

know how much_ I love_____ her._____

**Suddenly slower**

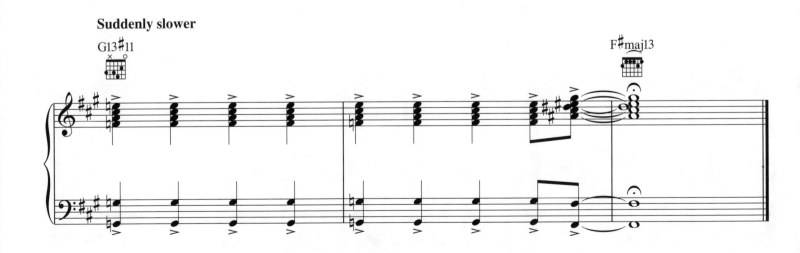